# Rail Power

## To Bernie O'Brien and Seth Corwin – the best locomotive crew I ever rode with.

First published in 2006 by Voyageur Press, an imprint of MBI Publishing Company, 400 First Avenue North, Suite 300, Minneapolis, MN 55401 USA

The information in this book is true and complete to the best of our knowledge. All recommendations are made without any guarantee on the part of the author or Publisher, who also disclaim any liability incurred in connection with the use of this data or specific details.

We recognize, further, that some words, model names, and designations mentioned herein are the property of the trademark holder. We use them for identification purposes only. This is not an official publication.

MBI Publishing Company titles are also available at discounts in bulk quantity for industrial or sales-promotional use. For details write to Special Sales Manager at MBI Publishing Company, 400 First Avenus North, Suite 300, Minneapolis, MN 55401 USA

ISBN-13: 978-0-7603-2547-6
ISBN-10: 0-7603-2547-2

Editor: Dennis Pernu
Designer: Maria Friedrich

Printed in China

*Front cover (main):* Built in 1927, Santa Fe No. 3751 was the first Northern constructed by Baldwin. Santa Fe ultimately purchased 65 4-8-4s. After World War II, as diesels took over passenger assignments, the 4-8-4s were bumped to freight service; all were retired by 1958.

*Title pages:* Distributed Power Units (DPUs) can be inserted either in the middle of a train or at the rear; in both cases, all the locomotives are controlled by the engineer in the lead locomotive. Here, Canadian Pacific AC4400CW No. 9666—a DPU—is running backward as it pushes a coal train into the Rockies.

## Author Bio

Steve Barry has had a lifelong interest in trains, beginning as a child in southern New Jersey. He graduated from Rutgers University in 1979 and has been contributing to the rail-hobby press for more than 20 years. In 1996 he left the accounting profession to start a new career by joining the staff of *Railfan & Railroad*. Steve will photograph anything on rails and when not shooting or writing, can be found in front of the TV watching *Star Trek* or NFL football. He also has a large collection of country music from the 1970s to the present, including 1,200 vinyl albums. Steve and his wife reside in Newton, New Jersey, with numerous cats and dogs.

# Contents

# Introduction

# Introduction

For almost two centuries, railroads have been intertwined with the history and development of North America. The westward growth of the United States was pushed by rail; British Columbia wouldn't become a Canadian province until twin ribbons of steel were in place across the Rocky Mountains.

From the start, there has been more than a little romanticism blended in with this history, and much of it lay in the magic of the locomotive. While boxcars and passenger coaches made the money, hauling goods and people from town to town, it was the locomotive that captured the imagination. Steam locomotives, which dominated the railroads for more than a century, were particularly romantic. Up close, they were powerful, noisy machines that seemed to be only barely controlled by the engineer. But from a distance, the mournful sound of a steam whistle echoing through the night captured the imagination of any dreamer.

Railroading seemed to lose a little of its romance with the passing of steam in the 1950s, but for anyone who cared to look, there was still a lot of excitement. Diesel locomotives, while not as imposing as their predecessors, became more and more powerful and their colorful paint schemes divided the railroad world into a rainbow it didn't have in the days of mostly black steam power. Meanwhile, electric locomotives became the epitome of

Perhaps the most quintessential electric locomotive of all time was the Raymond Loewy–designed GG1. By the mid-1960s, *Trains* magazine was warning of the stylish locomotive's demise. A few, however, continued in passenger service until the early 1980s.

high speed as they whisked trains between major metropolitan areas.

The most powerful man on any train is the conductor. It is he who dictates when a train moves and is responsible for ensuring the safe arrival of passengers and goods. But any boy who was asked what he wanted to be when he grew up—especially in the early twentieth century—would reply that he wanted to be an engineer. Taming the wild beast to obey your commands was the ultimate dream and the ultimate lure of rail power.

Southern Pacific's 4-8-4s were assigned the railroad's GS class, standing for either "general service" or "Golden State." Built by Lima in 1942, No. 4449 received streamlined skirting and Daylight passenger train colors (as did many of the SP's 4-8-4s).

One of the more unusual paint schemes to grace an F unit can be found on Verde Canyon FP7s No. 1510 and 1512, both built in 1953. The Verde Canyon operates tourist trains through a remote part of Arizona accessible only by rail.

# Steam
# Locomotives

# Steam Locomotives

Perhaps no piece of machinery has captured the American spirit as much as the steam locomotive. Early steam locomotives provided most people's first up-close encounters with the Industrial Age. Unlike other industries, railroads weren't hidden behind factory walls or buried deep in mines. Railroads—and steam locomotives—were no farther away than the edge of the station platform. And a steam locomotive had no secrets—all of its major moving parts were out in the open, at eye level, for everyone to see.

Colonel John Stevens operated the first steam locomotive in the United States, around a loop in his backyard in Hoboken, New Jersey. Locomotives of varying designs soon appeared all over the Eastern Seaboard. For the first half-century, locomotives remained small, because the maximum train length allowed by a locomotive's stopping power did not require the pulling power of a large engine. But with the implementation of the Westinghouse air brake, beginning in the late 1800s, braking was spread throughout the entire train. This allowed longer trains, which then necessitated increased power. Soon more driving wheels were added to locomotives, along with trailing trucks to provide more space for larger fireboxes.

As the number of locomotive types increased, Frederick Methven White developed a simple system that became the universal way to identify North American steam locomotives. White counted the pilot wheels ahead of the drivers, the drivers, and the wheels behind the drivers and put the numbers together with hyphens separating them. Thus, early locomotives with four pilot wheels, four drivers, and no trailing truck were identified as a 4-4-0. A third set of drivers added to the locomotive made it a 4-6-0. Putting a four-wheel trailing truck on a 4-6-0 produced a 4-6-4. The only deviation from the system was when the "Mallet" (pronounced *mal-lay*) locomotive type came about with two separate sets of drivers (complete with separate sets of cylinders). Each driver set was indicated separately, such as a 4-6-6-4 or 2-8-8-4.

Even though there was a standard for identifying basic locomotive types, classifying locomotives was anything but standard. In the Diesel Age, most railroads identified their locomotives by the manufacturers' model designations, but in the steam world every railroad classified their locomotives differently. Thus, even though all Northerns were 4-8-4s, the Union Pacific assigned them the FEF class, while Southern Pacific used GS, Reading had the T class, and on the Burlington Route it was the O class. And within classes, there were subclasses: for example, Southern Pacific had Northerns classified from GS1 through GS7.

Two major locomotive builders emerged at the dawn of the twentieth century. Baldwin Locomotive Works was started by Matthias W. Baldwin in 1832 and was based in the Philadelphia area. Baldwin was the dominate steam builder for most of its existence, but by the end of the Great Depression the company was in decline. It never became a major player in the diesel market, building its last steam locomotive in 1949 and ceasing to build large diesel locomotives in 1956 (small industrial locomotives were produced for a few more years).

Meanwhile, the American Locomotive Company (commonly called Alco) was formed in 1901 when eight small builders merged to compete with Baldwin. By 1929 Alco had united all its production in a plant in Schenectady, New York. Alco got into the diesel business in the 1920s and built its last steam locomotive in 1948.

Another player in steam construction was the Lima Locomotive Works of Lima, Ohio. Lima was a farm-machinery builder until Ephraim Shay sold the company his design for a locomotive suited for logging railroads in 1878. The construction of geared Shay locomotives led Lima to produce conventional power starting in 1911. Lima's big breakthrough occurred in 1922. While Baldwin and Alco experimented with high-pressure boilers and articulation to produce more power, Lima developed locomotives with large grate areas, a four-wheel trailing truck, large cylinders, lightweight side rods, and other improvements. These locomotives were not only more powerful, but also more efficient and became known as Lima "superpower." Lima merged with the General Machinery Corporation of Hamilton, Ohio, in 1947 to form Lima-Hamilton. In 1951 it merged with the struggling Baldwin to form Baldwin-Lima-Hamilton.

Steam production had all but stopped by 1950, and all three major builders tried to get into the diesel market. Alas, that market would be dominated by two new players: the Electro-Motive Division of General Motors (EMD) and General Electric. The steam builders, like their products, vanished into history.

*Previous pages:* The sunset for steam locomotives came in the 1950s as American railroads rushed to dieselize. By 1959 only a few hangers-on remained in Canada and Mexico. Nonetheless, for a century steam was the driving force as the New World expanded.

The first locomotive to pull a train in the United States was the *Best Friend of Charleston*, built by the West Point Foundry in New York in 1830. In June 1831 the boiler exploded when the fireman tied the steam safety valve shut. This replica was constructed in 1928.

John Stevens constructed the first steam locomotive in the United States in 1825 and operated it in his backyard in Hoboken, New Jersey. Many early locomotives had vertical boilers, such as the *Best Friend of Charleston*. By the early 1830s the horizontal boiler had gained favor.

*Left:* The *John Bull* was brought to the United States in pieces from England in 1831, where railroad pioneer John Stevens gave the "kit" to Isaac Dripps to assemble—with no drawings to work from. It entered service on the Camden & Amboy Railroad in New Jersey. The original *John Bull* survives, and a replica was constructed in 1939.

*Below:* The *John Molson* was one of Canada's earliest steam locomotives, imported from Scotland in 1849 and named for brewer John Molson, who financed the railroad. It operated on the Champlain & St. Lawrence Railroad in Quebec. This replica was built in 1970.

By the early 1850s, railroads had settled on the 4-4-0 configuration, as seen on the *Eureka*, built in 1875. The design became known as "American": four leading wheels allowed for less wear on the tracks on curves and four driving wheels provided enough power for trains of the time.

Both 4-4-0s present at Promontory, Utah, on May 10, 1869, were ultimately scrapped, but the National Park Service had replicas made in 1979 to commemorate the 110th anniversary of the Golden Spike. With no plans to work from, the locomotives were carefully designed from enlarged photos taken at Promontory.

*Left:* The Central Pacific's *Jupiter* was a fairly typical American type of the Civil War era. It was built in 1868 by the Schenectady Locomotive Works (a predecessor of the American Locomotive Company). The original *Jupiter* met its demise in 1909.

*Below:* Two 4-4-0s were present at the most famous event in North American railroad history: the driving of the Golden Spike at Promontory, Utah, on May 10, 1869. The *Jupiter* represented the Central Pacific and No. 119 represented the Union Pacific.

Pennsylvania Railroad No. 1223 was built at the line's Juniata Shops in Altoona, Pennsylvania, in 1909. At the peak of its popularity around 1875, the American type accounted for about 85 percent of all locomotives in service in the United States. By the time No. 1223 was built, they had been relegated to mostly branch line service.

Henry R. Campbell received a patent for the 4-4-0 locomotive in 1836, a mere five years after the *Best Friend of Charleston* became the first U.S.-built locomotive. *Railroad Gazette* assigned the name "American" to the type in 1872. Some 25,000 Americans had been built when the last left the factory floor in 1928.

*Left:* Baltimore & Ohio No. 25 was constructed by the Mason Machine Works in Massachusetts in 1856. It was completely rebuilt in 1926 and appeared in several movies including *The Great Locomotive Chase* and *The Wild, Wild West.*

*Below:* As the twentieth century began, 4-4-0s were still constructed, although heavier trains made them less useful. Built by Alco in 1909 for the Mississippi Central Railroad and today used on the Wilmington & Western in Delaware, No. 98 recalls railroading of a century ago.

Conway Scenic's No. 47 moves out of the roundhouse in Conway, New Hampshire. The 0-6-0 was homebuilt as No. 1795 by Grand Trunk Railway at its Point St. Charles Shop in Maine, and joined Canadian National's roster as No. 7470 when GT and CN merged.

Switchers are used for shuffling (switching) passenger and freight cars in yards. Steam-powered versions are usually identified by their lack of leading and trailing wheels and thus had wheel arrangements such as 0-4-0 and 0-8-0, with 0-6-0 being most common. Many steam switchers have found homes powering passenger trains on tourist railroads.

*Above:* Formerly Canadian National No. 7312, Strasburg Rail Road No. 31 still gets the call to haul an occasional load of freight. Built by Baldwin subsidiary Burnham, Williams & Co. in 1908, it served the Grand Trunk and CN before winding up in Pennsylvania.

*Left:* Switcher No. 26 was built by the Baldwin Locomotive Works in 1929 and served as the manufacturer's shop switcher in Eddystone, Pennsylvania, before being sold to Jackson Iron & Steel Company in 1948.

Canadian National No. 89 was one of several Moguls that operated on Ontario branch lines until 1958. They became the last 2-6-0s in regular service in North America. Light and not overly powerful, Moguls were at their best with short trains in flat countryside on minimally maintained branch lines.

The name Mogul probably comes from the fact that the 2-6-0s were more powerful than their contemporary 4-4-0s of the mid-1800s. In all, about 11,000 Moguls were built; most built after 1900 were for short lines, as large railroads had turned to more powerful loco-motives by then.

*Left:* When the first one appeared in the early 1860s, the 2-6-0 was the first steam locomotive to have a leading truck (wheel set) ahead of the drivers. The lead truck swiveled and created a three-point suspension, causing less stress.

*Below:* CN No. 89 was constructed in 1910, well after Moguls had peaked in popularity in the late 1800s. Although supplanted by Consolidations (2-8-0s) as the primary freight locomotive on most railroads, specialized service on branch lines kept Moguls in production until 1929.

Built by Baldwin in 1925 for service in South America, two Ten-Wheelers were repatriated to Walt Disney World in 1969 for theme park service. Disney World No. 1, the *Walter E. Disney*, gives a good idea of what a nineteenth-century Ten-Wheeler would have looked like.

**First appearing in the 1850s, Ten-Wheelers were originally built for freight service. Even with 2-8-0s and 2-8-2s as the dominant freight locomotives, Ten-Wheelers remained in production until almost 1930; by then, some 17,000 had been constructed.**

*Left:* The Ten-Wheeler evolved from the 4-4-0s of the mid-1800s. A third set of drivers made them more powerful, especially important as railroads expanded into the mountains. Ten-Wheelers generally had a narrow firebox that needed to sit between the driving wheels.

*Below:* Montreal Locomotive Works turned out No. 972 for the Canadian Pacific in 1912. CP kept its fleet of Ten-Wheelers active into the 1950s. Moderately sized drivers made them ideal for passenger and freight service requiring some power but not high speeds.

*Right:* Air pumps used to produce compressed air for braking are mounted on the front of Nevada Northern No. 93, shown at the railroad's shop in East Ely, Nevada; most locomotives had air pumps mounted on the sides. Air brakes allowed longer trains that required more powerful locomotives.

*Below:* A firebox mounted above the drivers rather than between them, as seen on Nevada Northern No. 93, provides more grate space for burning fuel, making for a more powerful locomotive. The trade-off is a smaller driver diameter, resulting in less speed.

The addition of a lead truck to 0-8-0s (making them Consolidation 2-8-0s) provided a three-point suspension. One point was the lead truck, which swiveled, while the sets of drivers on each side provided the other two points. This gave Consolidations a vastly superior ride over the rigid 0-8-0s and allowed higher speeds.

Nevada Northern No. 93 leads an ore train through the winter wonderland outside Ely, Nevada. Built at the American Locomotive Company's Pittsburgh plant in 1909, No. 93 has worked its entire life in Nevada, first hauling copper and later tourists.

Union Pacific No. 618 was built by Burnham, Williams & Co. in 1907. In 1958 it was retired and donated for display to Salt Lake City, which in turn donated it to the National Railway Historical Society in 1970. The Heber Valley Railroad later resurrected it for tourist service.

The Lehigh Valley took delivery of the first 2-8-0 in 1866 from Baldwin. The LV had completed a strategic merger with the Lehigh & Mahanoy and named its new 2-8-0 "Consolidation," a name that has been applied to every locomotive of that class ever since. Ultimately, 33,000 of the 2-8-0s were produced, more than any other steam-wheel arrangement.

*Left:* Consolidations survived on small railroads long after diesels had vanquished steam from the main lines. While not built for passenger service, many surviving 2-8-0s, like UP No. 618, have been resurrected by tourist railroads.

*Below:* Buffalo Creek & Gauley operated a small fleet of 2-8-0s in the West Virginia mountains into the 1960s. No. 14 was built by Alco in 1918. No. 14 ultimately ended up at the North Carolina Transportation Museum.

New Hope & Ivyland No. 40 presents a scene that comes straight out of 1940s southern railroading. No. 40 was built by Baldwin in 1925 for the Lancaster & Chester Railway in South Carolina. It later worked for the Cliffside Railroad in North Carolina until 1962.

Steam locomotives have been favorite subjects for photographers ever since the camera was invented. Many tourist railroads provide "photo freights," painting their locomotives (and often several freight cars) into paint schemes from the 1950s or earlier and running these special trains just for photographers.

*Left:* Western Maryland No. 734 was built by Baldwin in 1916 for the Lake Superior & Ishpeming Railroad in Michigan. It ultimately wound up on the Western Maryland Scenic Railroad, which painted the locomotive in a Western Maryland scheme.

*Below:* Helmstetter's Curve outside of Cumberland, Maryland, has been a favorite photo location for generations of railfans. Here, its namesake, John Helmstetter, looks on as Western Maryland No. 734 thunders around the curve that surrounds his property.

The H. K. Porter Company was one of the largest manufacturers of industrial locomotives, building almost 8,000 between 1866 and 1950. No. 65 was built in 1920 and worked for the Safe Harbor Water Power Company in Pennsylvania.

Tank locomotives had a "T" following their wheel arrangement designation (e.g., 0-6-0T); fireless cookers had an "F". Occasionally a locomotive had both a tank and a trailing tender, which required a designation such as 0-6-0T&T.

*Above:* While most tank engines had no lead or trailing trucks, some larger models sported both, such as 2-4-2T No. 5, built for logging service by Baldwin in 1906. No. 5 spent its entire life in New Hampshire.

*Left:* For working in tight spaces, some steam locomotives were built without tenders. Water was stored in tanks over the locomotive's boiler, while coal was stored in a small bunker behind the cab.

A cousin of the tank engine is the fireless cooker, used in industries with an ample available steam supply. Steam was simply pumped into the locomotive's boiler, and the locomotive ran until it needed a recharge. No. 6816 was built by Porter in 1923.

Fireless cookers had pressurized steam pumped into their boilers for fuel. The contained steam retained its heat well, only slowly cooling off enough to condense back into water, and therefore the pressure remained high enough to operate the locomotive for a couple of hours at a time.

*Left:* A "saddle tank" over the boiler to hold water is typical of tank locomotives. No. 43 was built by Vulcan Iron Works in Pennsylvania in 1918 and served a quarry in Connecticut.

*Below:* Fireless cookers served some power plants into the 1980s, including the Potomac Electric plant in Alexandria, Virginia, which used a Porter 0-4-0F built in 1949. Fireless cookers were also sometimes called "Thermos bottles."

Shays were the backbone of the Mower Lumber Company operation in West Virginia. When the company ceased harvesting timber, its trackage became the Cass Scenic Railroad where multiple Shays still climb Bald Knob.

Logging railroads usually ran on temporary track with little grading. As such, standard steam locomotives could not operate on them. Ephraim Shay developed a locomotive that was driven by vertical cylinders connected to a shaft that powered every axle. Lima Machine Works in Ohio built the first of Shay's locomotives and ultimately built almost 2,800 Shays between 1880 and 1944, making it the most-popular geared steam locomotive.

*Left:* A Shay built by Lima in 1923 brings a load of timber down from the mountains. Shays didn't go fast, but were very sure-footed on rough track and steep grades.

*Below:* Shay locomotives were well suited for logging railroads, where they ran on temporary track over uneven terrain. Ely-Thomas Lumber No. 6 was built in 1927 by Lima and worked in North Carolina and West Virginia.

Heisler locomotives also featured angled cylinders, but unlike a Climax, the Heisler's cylinders pointed inward to power a shaft running under the center of the locomotive. No. 6 was built in 1929 for service in West Virginia.

**Climax Manufacturing Company and Heisler Locomotive Works were both located in Pennsylvania. Climax production topped 1,000 locomotives between 1888 and 1928, while Heisler turned out over 600 locomotives between 1891 and 1941. Like Shays, Climaxes and Heislers had a shaft to deliver power to all axles.**

*Left:* With its cylinders and driveshaft mounted on one side of the locomotive, Shays featured an off-center boiler to equalize the weight. Shays could be found in the timberlands of the Pacific Northwest, New England, and the South.

*Below:* The inclined cylinders typical of a Climax locomotive are evident on No. 6, built in 1921 for timber service in New Hampshire. Today it hauls tourists through the White Mountains.

Manitou & Pikes Peak No. 4 was built in 1897 by Burnham, Williams & Company (Baldwin) to push tourists to the top of Pikes Peak. At 14,110 feet, the summit is the highest point in North America reachable by rail.

Cog railroads were seldom built for hauling freight—usually they were built as nineteenth-century tourist attractions. Two major cog railroads operate in North America: the Manitou & Pikes Peak Railway converted to diesel in the 1940s, while the Mount Washington Cog Railway remains 100 percent steam-powered.

*Left:* Cog railroads feature a rack rail between the two conventional rails; a cog wheel pulls the locomotive uphill on steep grades, and also assists in braking. Mount Washington Cog Railway, built in 1869, is the oldest cog railroad in the world.

*Below:* Mount Washington Cog Railway No. 3 climbs a 37 percent grade at Jacobs Ladder on its namesake New Hampshire mountain. The Manchester Locomotive Works built the engine in 1883. Mount Washington is 6,288 feet high.

New York, Susquehanna & Western No. 142 was one of the last three Mikados purchased for use in the United States, arriving fresh from the factory in China in 1988. All three locomotives were acquired by tourist railroads.

The Mikado got its unusual name when Baldwin built 2-8-2s for the Nippon Railway of Japan. The word Mikado (meaning "emperor of Japan") had just caught on in the United States thanks to the 1885 Gilbert & Sullivan opera *The Mikado*.

*Left:* The Mikado was a logical next step in steam power. By adding a trailing truck to a 2-8-0 (making a 2-8-2) the firebox no longer sat over the rear drivers, but rather sat lower over the trailing truck, allowing for a larger boiler with the same grate area as a Consolidation.

*Below:* Soo Line No. 1003 was built by Alco in 1913, one of ten ordered by the railroad that year. Like many other railroads during the first two decades of the twentieth century, the Soo Line purchased Mikados to replace Consolidations.

# MIKADO 2-8-2

The Chicago, Burlington & Quincy had 278 Mikados on its roster, starting with 60 from Baldwin in 1910. Some remained in service as late as 1957. CB&Q No. 4960 survived into the tourist train era, eventually winding up in Arizona on the Grand Canyon Railway.

From 1910 to 1919 the Mikado was the standard freight locomotive in the United States. Production fell off in the 1920s as larger locomotives were ordered to pull heavier trains. The last Mikado was ordered in 1948 for the Canadian Pacific Railway.

*Left:* While large railroads constantly upgraded their motive power to larger and faster engines, Mikados, like McCloud River No. 18 (Baldwin, 1918), were ideally suited for railroads where track conditions limited speed and locomotive weight.

*Below:* Canadian National No. 3254 was built by the Canadian Locomotive Company in 1917. The cylinder in front of the smokestack is a feedwater heater, used to preheat water before it is added to the locomotive's boiler.

The Denver & Rio Grande Western's narrow gauge empire ran into the 1960s, with Mikados such as No. 473 powering freight trains until the end. Two D&RGW narrow gauge remnants survived to become tourist railroads: the Durango & Silverton Narrow Gauge Railroad and the Cumbres & Toltec Scenic Railroad.

"Standard gauge" for most of the world's railroads is 4 feet 8 1/2 inches between rails. Anything narrower is considered "narrow gauge," the most common of which is 3 feet between rails. Some narrow gauge railroads, notably in Maine, had only 2 feet between rails.

*Left:* The Rio Grande operated the branch between Durango and Silverton, Colorado, for tourist service into the 1970s. The line was eventually sold to the Durango & Silverton Narrow Gauge Railroad, which upgraded the tracks for heavier K-36s and K-37s.

*Below:* The Rio Grande had four classes of narrow gauge 2-8-2s. The K-27s, built in 1903, were the lightest. The K-28s followed in 1923, with the K-36s and K-37s following in 1925 and 1928. No. 487 is a K-36.

While Colorado narrow gauge is certainly the most famous, another 3-foot line operated in the Pennsylvania coalfields. The East Broad Top relied on six Baldwin-built Mikados (such as No. 17, built in 1918) to power its trains.

During World War II, several railroads tried to change the designation of their 2-8-2s from "Mikados" to "MacArthurs" in honor of the U.S. general. Suffice to say, the name change never stuck.

*Left:* The Rio Grande painted Mikado No. 473 in its "bumblebee" scheme in the 1950s, and Durango & Silverton revived the livery in 2003. The beauty of Colorado's Animas River Valley kept the Silverton Branch running long after most of the Rio Grande's narrow gauge empire was abandoned.

*Below:* Four of the East Broad Top's six Mikados were used in tourist service after the line ceased hauling revenue freight in 1956. No. 15, built in 1914, recreates a scene from its coal-hauling days almost a half-century later.

As diesels took over the main lines in the 1940s and 1950s, most steam locomotives met with the scrapper's torch. Fate would be kind to Norfolk & Western 4-8-0 No. 1118, though, which was rescued by a museum after half a century on the scrap line.

The Twelve-Wheeler was a short-lived design, with only about 600 produced (Norfolk & Western had almost half of the entire production). Originally envisioned as an improvement on the Consolidation (a longer wheelbase allowed a bigger boiler), it was replaced by the Mikado. Only six Twelve-Wheelers were built after World War I.

*Above:* Norfolk & Western had the largest fleet of Twelve-Wheelers, purchasing 286 between 1906 and 1911. A handful survived right up to the end of steam in 1958, working branch lines in Virginia. No. 475 ended up in Pennsylvania on the Strasburg Rail Road.

*Left:* Strasburg Rail Road No. 475, built by Baldwin in 1907, started life as a branch line freight locomotive on the Norfolk & Western. Retired by the N&W in 1958, No. 475 has enjoyed a second life hauling tourists through Pennsylvania's Dutch country.

Decapod No. 90 shows off its lanky profile as it runs on the Strasburg Rail Road. Baldwin built its Decapods in two weights: No. 90 weighs 106 tons; the heavier Baldwins weighed 125 tons. No. 90 was built in 1924 to haul sugar beets in Colorado.

The Pennsylvania Railroad was a believer in the Decapod, and it designed a monster locomotive that weighed 193 tons. The Pennsy built 123 Decapods in its own shop between 1918 and 1919, and had Baldwin build another 475 in 1922 and 1923.

*Left:* In all, six railroads purchased 22 of Baldwin's light Decapods; No. 90 was the only one purchased by the Great Western Railroad. Baldwin sold 21 of its heavier Decapods to two railroads.

*Below:* Frisco No. 1630 was one of 1,057 Decapods built for the Russian government during World War I. The Bolshevik Revolution in 1917 resulted in the order's cancellation, and the 200 remaining Decapods were allocated to U.S. railroads for the war effort.

*Above:* Pennsylvania Railroad No. 7002 recorded the fastest speed ever achieved by a steam locomotive when it reached 127.1 mph in 1905. The Pennsy was slow to replace the Atlantic with the larger Pacifics, and was still purchasing Atlantics until 1913.

*Right:* With their large driving wheels, Atlantics had a lot of speed but little traction. The introduction of steel passenger cars in the early 1900s made for heavier trains, and most railroads turned to 4-6-2 Pacifics.

When railroads started running faster passenger trains in the 1890s, they needed a high-horsepower locomotive for quicker starts. This was achieved by adding a trailing truck to the 4-4-0 American design, creating 4-4-2 Atlantics. The trailing truck allowed for a larger boiler. About 1,900 Atlantics were constructed.

After No. 7002 achieved its speed record in 1905, it was sent to the scrap yard. Somewhat embarrassed, the PRR resurrected No. 7002 for the Chicago World's Fair in 1949 by modifying Atlantic No. 8063 as a stand-in.

Perhaps the most famous Pacifics ever built were the Pennsylvania Railroad's class K4. Some 424 units were built between 1917 and 1928. Preserved K4 No. 1351 became Pennsylvania's official state steam locomotive in the 1990s.

The Pacific was a natural progression from the Atlantic 4-4-2. The added set of driving wheels allowed the locomotives to pull longer trains, and the additional weight provided more traction. Mass production of Pacifics ceased by 1930, with Hudsons becoming the preferred passenger power.

*Left:* Canadian Pacific 4-6-2s, used in commuter service out of Montreal until the late 1950s, were some North America's last passenger steam in regular service. One of the last Pacifics built, CP No. 1293 came from the Canadian Locomotive Company in 1948.

*Below:* Louisville & Nashville No. 152, built by Rogers Locomotive Works in 1905, was one of the lighter Pacifics at 94 tons. With their high drivers, light Pacifics were some of the most graceful-looking steam locomotives ever built.

Canadian Pacific rostered 398 Pacifics built between 1906 and 1948. After most railroads had moved to Hudsons for passenger power, CP had 224 4-6-2s built between 1938 and 1948 to replace ancient Ten-Wheelers on branch line passenger trains.

Pacifics first appeared in the late 1800s and were simply Ten-Wheelers with an axle under the cab, retaining the 4-6-0's narrow firebox between the drivers. The first Pacifics with a wide firebox over the trailing truck were built for the Missouri Pacific in 1902.

*Left:* At 158 tons, CPR No. 2317, built in 1923 by the Montreal Locomotive Works, was among the heaviest Pacifics constructed. No. 2317 found a new home working at Steamtown U.S.A.

*Below:* The U.S. rail preservation movement was getting underway in the early 1960s, as CPR retired the last of the Pacifics. Millionaire Nelson Blount purchased five CPR Pacifics (and spare parts) for his Steamtown U.S.A. museum in Vermont.

Canadian Pacific 4-6-4 No. 2816 was built by Montreal Locomotive Works in 1930. After going to the Steamtown museum in the 1960s, it was repatriated by CPR in 1998 to operate on business trains and excursions for its original owner.

Of the 487 Hudsons built between 1927 and 1948, New York Central had the most with 275. In the 1950s, most railroads assigned their new diesels to heavy passenger trains, the domain of Hudsons. Too heavy for branch lines and not suited for freight service, many Hudsons had very short careers before being scrapped. None of NYC's Hudsons (considered by some to be the best-designed locomotives ever) were saved.

*Above:* In the late 1920s, CPR looked at purchasing 4-8-4 Northerns to power heavy passenger trains. After receiving just two Northerns, CPR decided the locomotives were too heavy and commissioned 65 Hudsons, the second largest fleet in North America.

*Left:* CPR had 40 Hudsons built with streamlining. In 1939 No. 2850 was assigned to pull a train carrying King George VI and Queen Elizabeth across Canada. Eventually all 40 streamlined Hudsons, including No. 2839, had royal crowns applied to their sides and became known as "Royal Hudsons."

61

Nickel Plate Road No. 765 was built by Lima in 1944 for fast freight service along Lake Erie. Lima 2-8-4s were among the best pure freight locomotives ever constructed, with large grates slung over a four-wheel trailing truck.

The first 2-8-4 tested on New York Central subsidiary Boston & Albany in the Berkshire Mountains (hence the name). The fast-running freight locomotive was an instant success, with the B&A buying 45. The Van Sweringen railroads' Unified Advisory Committee took the design to its ultimate success when it designed 2-8-4s for the Nickel Plate in 1934. Production of Berkshires ended in 1949 with 611 locomotives built.

*Left:* Built in 1941, No. 1225 was one of 40 Berkshires purchased by the Pere Marquette. It's greatest claim to fame, however, might be that it was the pattern for the locomotive in the computer-generated movie *The Polar Express.*

*Below:* The Van Sweringen brothers controlled the Nickel Plate, as well as the Erie; Chesapeake & Ohio; Pere Marquette; and Wheeling & Lake Erie. All five railroads ultimately received Berkshires similar to those of the Nickel Plate. Pere Marquette's 2-8-4s had slightly larger cylinders than Nickel Plate's.

The St. Louis–San Francisco Railway (Frisco) purchased 4-8-2s to run in the Ozark Mountains on passenger trains that previously required two Pacifics. Frisco No. 1522 was built by Baldwin in 1926. Light by Mountain standards, No. 1522 weighs 171 tons.

The first Mountains were built for the Chesapeake & Ohio in 1910 to replace 4-6-2s on passenger trains. The western roads used them on long-distance passenger trains, while the eastern railroads used them for fast freight service. Some railroads, such as the Canadian National and New York Central, used them in both capacities.

*Above:* Canadian National purchased Mountains for both passenger and freight service. No. 6060 was built in 1944 by the Montreal Locomotive Works, one of the last 20 Mountains purchased by CN. The group was semistreamlined, leading to the nickname "Bullet-Nosed Bettys."

*Left:* Developed first as a passenger locomotive, the Mountain had eight drivers that gave the type a lot of power for freight. Even after the advent of the larger 4-8-4 Northern, many railroads continued to purchase Mountains. In all, over 2,200 were built.

In all, Chesapeake & Ohio purchased 12 superpower 4-8-4s they called Greenbriars from Lima. No. 614 was purchased in 1948 just as the diesel age was beginning. By 1952 the Greenbriars had been retired, although three were called back for a traffic surge in 1955.

The first 4-8-4s were purchased by the Great Northern from Alco in 1926 and 1927. Originally called "Northern Pacific" types, the name was later shortened. The ultimate combination of speed, power, and design, Northerns were the pinnacle of non-articulated steam development.

*Left:* Needing fast freight power during World War II, the Reading rebuilt 30 Consolidations into Northerns from 1945 to 1947. Four of the Northerns received national acclaim when the Reading saved them for passenger excursion service in the early 1960s.

*Below:* The Milwaukee Road purchased ten Northerns from Alco in 1944 for dual service. Classified as S3s, the Northerns were shorter than their 42 predecessor 4-8-4s, allowing them to pull passenger trains into the tight clearances of Chicago's Union Station.

*Right:* The St. Louis South-western (Cotton Belt) made a leap from mostly Consolidations to Northerns without an intermediate locomotive type. Cotton Belt No. 819 was the last of the road's 20 Northerns, homebuilt by the railroad in 1942.

*Below:* Between 1941 and 1950, Norfolk & Western built 14 4-8-4s in their Roanoke, Virginia, shops. Assigned the J class, the locomotives were never referred to as Northerns. Used on passenger trains, No. 611 served only a decade before dieselization forced retirement.

The 4-8-4 wheel arrangement had the most names of any steam type. While most railroads called them Northerns, southern railroads had other ideas, variously calling them Dixies, Potomacs, and Greenbriers. Other railroads called their 4-8-4s Poconos and Niagaras.

In 1927 Canadian National ordered 160 Northerns for its own lines and 43 for subsidiary Grand Trunk. No. 6325 was built by Alco in 1942; like all of CN's Northerns (and Mountains), it was used in both freight and passenger service.

In its second career as a fan trip locomotive, Union Pacific 8444 (844) lays down a plume of oil smoke for photographers during an excursion for the National Railway Historical Society. A properly fired steam locomotive seldom smoked this much.

Union Pacific No. 844 is the only steam locomotive owned by a major North American railroad but never retired. After just a decade in regular service, 844 now has logged over 40 years of excursion service.

*Above:* Through 1980s mergers, Union Pacific No. 844 wound up in territory not historically associated with the UP. The merger with the Southern Pacific and its subsidiary Cotton Belt allowed No. 844 to share St. Louis Union Station with Cotton Belt No. 819.

*Left:* UP No. 844 was built by Alco in 1944, the last of 45 Northerns purchased. It was used on passenger trains until the late 1950s. The UP's Northerns were designed to work comfortably on long stretches of prairie with interspersed mountain grades.

Texas & Pacific No. 610 was one of the first 2-10-4s ever built (T&P purchased 10 in 1925; No. 610 came with a second purchase of 15 in 1927). With low drivers, the locomotive was not suited for passenger work but could certainly lug heavy freights.

Lima Locomotive Works created the Texas type by stretching its 2-8-4s and adding a fifth set of drivers. The heavy freights the Texas types were assigned to were some of the first the railroads wanted to dieselize, so the 2-10-4s were among the first freight steam locomotives retired. From 1925 until 1949, over 400 2-10-4s were constructed.

*Left:* T&P No. 610 was a member of perhaps the most famous group of Texas types, but other railroads had more. The T&P purchased 70 2-10-4s between 1925 and 1929. By comparison, the Pennsylvania Railroad had 125.

*Below:* No. 610 was equipped with a distinctive feedwater heater, built by Elesco, above its brow. Water from the tender ran into the heater to be preheated by the locomotive's exhaust before being put into the boiler.

Norfolk & Western No. 1218 was among the finest 2-6-6-4s ever built. N&W constructed 43 of the massive locomotives in its own shop between 1936 and 1950. The A's could handle passenger trains, fast freight, and coal trains in the West Virginia mountains.

Articulated locomotives solved the problem of increasing locomotive power while keeping the wheelbase flexible. The 2-6-6-4 was the first design to put the firebox entirely over the trailing truck, allowing for larger drivers, a deeper firebox, and increased speed and horsepower. The first 2-6-6-4s were built for the Pittsburgh & West Virginia in 1934.

*Above:* Two sets of drivers allowed articulated locomotives to negotiate curves that locomotives with ten coupled drivers couldn't. The rear set of drivers was attached to the locomotive's frame and boiler. The front set of drivers swiveled under the locomotive's frame and the front cylinders used steam that had been exhausted from the rear cylinders.

*Left:* N&W No. 1218 was retired in the late 1950s, but the N&W's merger with the Southern Railway in the mid-1980s gave it new life. The Southern had a popular steam excursion program, and the Norfolk Southern Railway continued the tradition until 1996.

In 1992 the Clinchfield leased Union Pacific No. 3985 to power the fiftieth running of its *Santa Claus Train*. It ran through Appalachia disguised as Clinchfield No. 676 (the last of Clinchfield's 18 Challengers was numbered 675).

With 69- or 70-inch drivers, the Challenger was capable of high speeds. Union Pacific bought the first 4-6-6-4 in 1936, about the same time it was introducing its Challenger passenger train. A total of 252 Challengers were built. Most buyers used them exclusively in high-speed freight service, but UP used them in passenger service as well.

*Left:* Ever mindful of its history, UP stored Challenger No. 3985 in its roundhouse in Cheyenne, Wyoming, after the locomotive was retired. Eventually it was put on display, but in 1981 UP restored the 4-6-6-4 to power excursions and corporate trains.

*Below:* The UP designed the Challenger to replace 4-12-2s, whose long rigid wheelbases didn't allow for large drivers. The Challenger was essentially a 4-12-2 with the drivers split by articulation, plus a four-wheel trailing truck to accommodate a larger firebox.

# Electric
# Locomotives

# Electric Locomotives

The full potential of electrified railroads was never achieved in North America, despite a promising beginning. Once the leader in electrified miles of trackage, the United States now has only a handful of major lines using electricity, most of which are commuter operations.

In 1880, Thomas Alva Edison developed an electric locomotive capable of reaching 40 mph, and the groundwork for a major changeover from steam to electrified rail power was set. Then, in 1895, Frank J. Sprague invented a system that allowed multiple locomotives to be operated by one crew from one cab—something that was impossible with steam locomotives. Multiple-unit technology was quickly implemented on elevated mass transit lines, and it became apparent that electric locomotives could be grouped to pull longer trains on the main line railroads at a substantial savings over steam power.

The Baltimore & Ohio was the first of the steam railroads to experiment with main line electrification. At the B&O's Mount Royal station in Baltimore, trains departing southward immediately entered a tunnel under the city's streets. Steam power, and its associated smoke (especially while accelerating out of a station), was impractical, so the B&O electrified the tunnel. A lone electric locomotive would pull the entire train, including the steam locomotive, through the tunnel.

Still, main line electrification was slow in coming. Many railroads instituted short stretches (under 100 miles in length) to tackle heavy grades that included tunnels. The Great Northern put up wires over 70 miles of track leading up to Cascade Tunnel in Washington State. Likewise, the Norfolk & Western electrified its line out of Bluefield, West Virginia, for 30 miles to and through Elkhorn Tunnel.

During this time, two major suppliers of electric locomotives and infrastructure emerged. General Electric was the leader in supplying direct current (DC) equipment, which allowed for simple locomotives but required a complex energy delivery system. Westinghouse went with alternating current

(AC), which cost less to install but required more complex locomotives.

Electrification was embraced by the commuter railroads early on, nudged along by an ordinance that barred steam locomotives within New York City by 1908. The New York Central electrified its line into Grand Central Terminal. The Pennsylvania Railroad dug its tunnels under the Hudson River from New Jersey, and soon all trains entered Manhattan after changing from steam power to electric at Manhattan Transfer. The Long Island Rail Road, a subsidiary of the Pennsylvania, also electrified, using a third rail (instead of the more common overhead wire) to supply power.

The Chicago, Milwaukee, St. Paul & Pacific (the Milwaukee Road) was the first to install main line electrification over a vast distance. On its 1,780-mile route between St. Paul and Seattle, wire was strung over 646 miles. Electrification started in Harlowton, Montana, and went to Avery, Idaho. At that point there was a 235-mile gap in the wires, which picked up again in Othello, Washington, and ended in Tacoma.

The most famous and most enduring main line electrification was started in 1929. The mighty Pennsylvania Railroad, seemingly immune to the Great Depression that gripped the United States, embarked on a project to rebuild and electrify its main line from New York to Washington, D.C. To operate the line, the railroad designed and constructed the GG1 locomotive, the most famous of all North American electrics.

Chicago and Philadelphia ultimately saw electrified commuter service, along with New York City. But all of the commuter lines in Chicago and Philadelphia, as well as the bulk of the commuter lines serving New York City, did not see locomotives developed for the service. Instead, multiple-unit passenger cars (basically self-propelled coaches) became the backbone for getting people to and from work.

The advent of the diesel-electric brought an end to many electrified operations. Diesels didn't smoke as much as steam locomotives, eliminating the problems with all but the longest tunnels, and could be run in multiple-unit sets by one crew at a substantial savings over steam power, just like electrics. But diesels also had a few key advantages over electrics: if a railroad experienced a downturn in traffic, diesel power could be sold off or leased out to any other railroad, unlike specialized electric locomotives, and diesels didn't bring with them all the maintenance that overhead wires required. By the 1960s, electrification had retrenched to the commuter railroads, the Pennsylvania Railroad lines, and the Milwaukee Road. The Milwaukee cut the power in 1974, ending the last main line electrification that was primarily for freight.

*Previous page:* Amtrak AEM7 No. 944 rolls south from Wilmington, Delaware, with a typical consist of Amfleet cars. From 1981 onward, AEM7s were Amtrak's premier electric motive power.

Iowa Traction Company Nos. 50 and 54 still work in daily freight service in Mason City, Iowa. Both were built by Baldwin and Westinghouse: No. 50 in 1920 for the Washington & Old Dominion; No. 54 in 1923 for Iowa Southern Utilities.

The four locomotives of the Iowa Traction Company are the oldest electric locomotives still in daily service in North America. The newest locomotive was built in 1923.

*Left:* Many early electric locomotives were built for streetcar lines that also provided freight service. Built by Westinghouse in 1930, Sacramento Northern X654 served until the railroad went all diesel in 1965.

*Below:* Constructed by Alco and GE in 1922, Yakima Valley Transportation Company No. 298 provided freight service over the streetcar lines of Yakima, Washington.

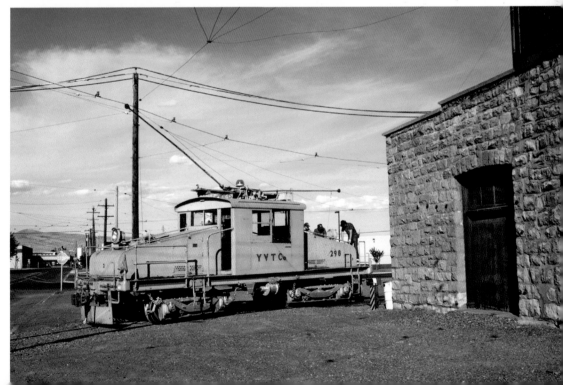

Two of the three steeplecabs built for CN by GE in 1950 wait to head into Montreal. Their rapid acceleration made them crew favorites. CN classified them as model Z-5a.

Of CN's 18 electric locomotives used in Montreal service, 13 remained until 1995 when the line was upgraded and all remaining motors were retired. All nine of the British boxcabs were scrapped, as were the three GE steeplecabs. Five of the six GE boxcabs were preserved by museums.

*Left:* British-built Canadian National boxcab No. 6722 pulls a diesel-powered passenger train clear of the 1.5-mile Mount Royal Tunnel after departing Montreal's Central Station.

*Below:* Canadian National boxcab No. 6723 and eight sister locomotives were built by Beyer Peacock of Great Britain between 1924 and 1926, and were brought to Canada in 1941 to supplement six GE-built boxcabs already working the Mount Royal Tunnel.

# GG1: THE BEST EVER BUILT

No. 4877, leading a commuter train across the Raritan Bay in New Jersey, was one of 139 GG1 locomotives built for the Pennsylvania Railroad between 1935 and 1943 by a consortium including GE, Westinghouse, Baldwin, and the PRR shops in Altoona, Pennsylvania.

Raymond Loewy, a noted industrial designer, came up with the idea of giving the GG1 the welded skin that made it a favorite among aficionados of industrial design. Loewy also designed the T-1 locomotive, Studebaker automobiles, Lucky Strike cigarette packaging, and more.

*Left:* The GG1 outlived the Pennsylvania Railroad. No. 4881 lost its Pennsy pinstripes for basic black and worked for the New Jersey DOT in commuter service. Other GG1s went to Conrail and Amtrak.

*Below:* GG1 No. 4859 sits under the Harrisburg, Pennsylvania, train shed, the farthest point west reached by the Pennsylvania's wires. Sharing the shed is a multiple-unit Metroliner, the model that supplanted the GG1 in high-speed New York–Washington service.

An all-steel frame and extra weight (thanks to added concrete ballast) also allowed the GG1s to handle heavy freight loads. The complete package of grace, speed, and brute strength, most GG1s provided more than 40 years of service.

On January 14, 1953, GG1 No. 4876 had a brake failure while approaching Washington Union Station. The locomotive and train crashed through the end of the station platform and No. 4876 slid across the station concourse until the floor gave way and it fell into the station's basement. There were 87 injuries; amazingly, no one was killed. No. 4876 was cut into three pieces, lifted out of the station, and reassembled to become one of the last GG1s in active service.

*Above:* The PRR painted GG1s in two basic colors: Brunswick green (such as on the 4859) and Tuscan red. A few were painted silver for service on the all-stainless-steel *Congressional Limited.* The "cat whisker" pinstripes were later traded for a single wide yellow stripe.

*Left:* A southbound GG1 races through New Jersey after departing New York City. The GG1 allowed for faster times between New York and Washington than steam could ever accomplish and eliminated an engine change for the run in the Hudson River tunnels.

Pennsylvania Railroad No. 4935, in service for Amtrak, rumbles across the Susquehanna River en route to New York City. Plans to change the Northeast Corridor from 25 Hz to 60 Hz finally forced the GG1s out. The change never occurred, leading one to wonder if the GG1s could have made it into the twenty-first century.

By the late 1970s, GG1s had been withdrawn from freight service. As a tribute, Amtrak painted No. 4935 in Brunswick green, while New Jersey Transit painted No. 4877 in Tuscan red. Amtrak retired its last GG1 in 1981; NJT did the same in 1983.

*Left:* The Swedish-designed AEM7 replaced the GG1. After working for the Pennsylvania Railroad and its successors—Penn Central, Conrail, Amtrak, and New Jersey Transit—the last GG1s were retired in 1983.

*Below:* Ivy City engine terminal, just north of Washington's Union Station, was the southern terminal for the GG1s. In its waning days, No. 4935 shares track with E60 No. 968 and GG1 No. 4872, which sports the black paint most GG1s wore late in their careers.

After Amtrak deemed the E60s a failure for high-speed intercity service, New Jersey Transit purchased six of them for service to the New Jersey seashore communities. The commuter service hardly taxed the 6,000-horsepower locomotives.

Designed for 120-mph running, the E60 failed miserably in testing and was relegated to slower service, leaving Amtrak's fastest trains in the capable hands of aging GG1s. Amtrak scheduled complete rebuilds of several E60s in 2003, but ordered them scrapped midway through the overhauls. Two have been preserved by museums.

*Left:* Built from 1974 to 1976, the first new electric power purchased by Amtrak, came in two versions: the E60CP had steam generators to supply steam heat to older cars, while the E60CH had "head-end power" generators to supply juice to new Amfleet cars. Here, No. 953, powers a southbound train from New York City.

*Below:* E60 No. 600, which will be replaced by a diesel in Washington, D.C., proves more than capable of handling a heavy Florida-bound Amtrak train. E60s stayed in service until 2003, powering long, slightly slower (by Northeast Corridor standards) trains. Ultimately, the arrival of the HHP8s made the E60s redundant.

Amtrak No. 905 was one of 53 AEM7s purchased starting in 1979. Based on a Swedish design, they were built by Electro-Motive Division (EMD) with a top speed of 125 mph and 7,000 horsepower.

AEM7s have had a couple of nicknames: "Swedish meatballs," referring to their origin and their compact profile compared to the GG1 and E60, and, more commonly, "toaster," because they look like a silver toaster when viewed broadside.

*Left:* The Southeastern Pennsylvania Transportation Authority purchased seven AEM7s in 1983 to provide express service, primarily on the ex–Pennsylvania Railroad line between Philadelphia and Paoli.

*Below:* AEM7s can travel at 125 mph when pulling trains on a Metroliner schedule, 110 mph when working a regional schedule with more frequent stops, and 90 mph when assigned to heavier long-distance trains. Two AEM7s are used on trains longer than eight cars.

Maryland Area Rail Commuter (MARC) purchased five AEM7s in 1986 and placed them in service between Baltimore and Washington. Each November, MARC's AEM7s are leased to Amtrak for use far from the Northeast Corridor.

With the exception of the high-end Acela trains, new electric locomotives have been based on technology that was proven by the AEM7. The ALP44 and ALP46 locomotives are largely AEM7s with slight upgrading.

*Left:* The AEM7s' boxy bodies were built by the Budd Company, noted for its production of stainless-steel passenger cars during the streamlined era. Budd is located in suburban Philadelphia, not far from the tracks where the AEM7s would ultimately work.

*Below:* Acelas have replaced the Metroliners on the fastest schedules, but AEM7s still reign over regional trains, despite the subsequent arrival of the HHP8. In 1999, the AEM7s entered a rebuilding program, ensuring they will remain Amtrak's workhorses for years to come.

# ALP44: THE AEM7'S COMMUTER COUSIN

New Jersey Transit ALP44 No. 4424 was imported from ASEA Brown Boveri of Sweden in 1996. NJT's former Delaware, Lackawanna & Western commuter lines, originally electrified in the 1930s, were always the domain of multiple-unit passenger equipment; the ALP44s became the first electric locomotives ever used on the lines.

The ALP44 has proven so reliable that NJT has decided to gradually eliminate multiple-unit passenger equipment in favor of locomotive-hauled trains. Local railfans refer to the ALP44s as "raccoons" for obvious reasons.

*Above:* The ALP44s were NJT's first new electric locomotives; until their arrival, NJT had made due with well-worn, hand-me-down GG1s and E60s. No. 4402 was one of 15 to arrive in 1990; another 18 followed between 1995 and 1997.

*Left:* ALP44s have worked alongside AEM7s on Amtrak's Northeast Corridor, where NJT provides local service. While AEM7s were assembled in the United States, the ALP44s were imported from Sweden. The only reason NJT didn't purchase AEM7s was because EMD had ceased production of the model.

A German-built ICE (Inter-City Express) train passes the Philadelphia skyline during testing in 1994. Crews were generally impressed with the power and acceleration of Siemens' entry in the bidding to build Amtrak's new generation of high-speed trains.

Bombardier entered the bidding for Amtrak's high-speed trains as the exclusive licensee to French TGV technology. Although the Canadian manufacturer did not provide a test train, it was the winning bidder. It all came down to an attractive financing offer.

*Left:* Built by ASEA Brown Boveri, the X2000 was a test-bed for the Swedish company's bid to manufacture Amtrak's high-speed trains for the twenty-first century. X2000 cars tilt inward on curves, minimizing the effect of centrifugal forces and allowing higher speeds.

*Below:* The ICE test train featured a bistro car that proved quite popular with passengers who rode it in regular Amtrak service.

As part of a massive Northeast Corridor improvement in the late 1990s, electrification was extended from New Haven to Boston, and Amtrak purchased 15 HHP8s from Bombardier between 1998 and 2001 to supplement its AEM7s.

An HHP8 is of much the same design as an Acela power unit, also built by Bombardier, but has cabs at both ends of the locomotive (an Acela power car is semipermanently coupled to the passenger car behind it) and 2,000 more horsepower than an Acela.

*Above:* HHP8s are rated for a top speed of 135 mph and pack 2,000 more horsepower than an AEM7. However, since HHP8s and AEM7s are used interchangeably, the HHP8s are usually assigned to trains that require a top speed of just 125 mph or less.

*Left:* While the AEM7s look like rolling kitchen appliances, the HHP8s have sleek European-style noses. Like most electric locomotives, the HHP8s are equipped with dual cabs so they don't have to be turned at each end of the railroad.

Amtrak's Acela train sets entered service in December 2000 amid much fanfare. The sleek trains, each six cars long with a power unit at each end, are capable of a top speed of 150 mph. Amtrak purchased 20 complete Acela sets.

While Bombardier based the Acela design on French TGV technology, only the traction components and truck (wheel) technology came directly from TGV. The rest was based on proven technologies from other sources—no new groundbreaking designs went into the trains.

*Left:* While an Acela power car is rated 2,000 at horsepower less than an HHP8 (6,000 versus 8,000), each set has two, providing 12,000 horsepower. Each train has four business cars, a café car, and a bistro car.

An Acela passes unused Holmesburg Prison in Philadelphia. The Acela's top speed of 150 mph cuts New York–to–Washington travel time from 3 hours to 2 hours and 45 minutes, a big savings when competing with air shuttles and automobiles.

The 660-foot Acelas were designed to allow the passenger cars to lean inward on curves, minimizing the effect of centrifugal forces and allowing greater speeds.

The Acela name was created for Amtrak by a marketing firm, reflecting a combination of acceleration and excellence. Bombardier built the trains entirely in U.S. plants at Barre, Vermont, and Plattsburgh, New York.

*Left:* Catenary wire installed by the New Haven Railroad in the 1930s was still being used when the Acelas entered service. As part of the Northeast Corridor improvement, the entire electric supply system between Washington and New Haven was upgraded and electrification was extended to Boston.

*Below:* One goal of the Acela program was to trim New York–to–Boston running times to less than 3 1/2 hours. Acela has beat that goal by 7 minutes.

# Diesel Locomotives

# Diesel Locomotives

The diesel locomotive was the single most important technological development in twentieth century railroading (actually, the locomotives are diesel-electrics; a diesel powerplant generates electricity, which in turn powers the traction motors). Introduced in mass production in 1939, by the mid-1950s diesels had all but eliminated steam from the major U.S. and Canadian railways.

Diesel railroad applications date as far back as 1918, to experimental units developed by General Electric. A crucial event in diesel development occurred in 1933, when the Budd Company was designing a lightweight articulated passenger train. Needing a prime mover, Budd took a fancy to the experimental Winton 201-A (Winton and the Electro-Motive Engineering Company had three years earlier become subsidiaries of General Motors under the name Electro-Motive Corporation). The result was the *Pioneer Zephyr*, which in 1934 dashed between Denver and Chicago in just 14 hours. EMC went on to develop the EMC 567, a V-configured engine that was produced

in sizes from 6 cylinders to 16 cylinders and remained standard power for locomotives until 1965.

As demand grew for a diesel locomotive that could power conventional trains, EMC (which would be fully merged into GM in 1941 as the Electro-Motive Division) introduced the FT. A semipermanently coupled pair of locomotives, the FT could produce 2,700 horsepower and, while using just one crew, be combined with any number of units to produce whatever power was necessary.

EMD caught a major break in 1941, when the U.S. War Production Board suspended the development of new locomotives. With the only proven diesel design, EMD spent the next four years perfecting its products while Alco, Lima, and Baldwin were required to continue producing steam locomotives. Lima and Baldwin merged in 1950, but the combined company ceased business in 1956. Fairbanks-Morse jumped into the market in 1944 and produced its last locomotive for a U.S. railroad in 1958. Alco, however, continued its competition with EMD.

EMD's products dominated the 1950s marketplace with its four-axle GP and six-axle SD freight locomotives and with its line of F and E cab units. Over 50,000 steam locomotives were sidelined, replaced by about 25,000 diesels.

Horsepower inched upward to 2,000 in the 1950s. Then, in 1958, EMD offered its first turbocharged locomotive, the 2,400-horsepower SD24. A turbine powered by the stream of exhaust gases increased air pressure in the cylinders, allowing an increase of fuel introduced into the cylinders. The 16-cylinder 567 powerplant produced 1,800 horsepower without turbocharging and 2,400 with it.

General Electric, a supplier of railroad traction equipment since 1925, had joined into a marketing agreement with Alco in 1940. In 1953, however, GE began to develop its own locomotives, but wouldn't become a major player until 1960 when it introduced the U25B. The Universal Series (called U-boats) soon surpassed Alco's Century series, and GE rapidly became the number-two manufacturer. Alco would throw in the towel in 1969.

A serious battle for horsepower developed. EMD replaced its long-lived 567 engine with the 645 in 1966. EMD's Dash 2 series, starting with the SD40-2 in 1972, introduced microprocessors. GE responded with its Dash 7 series. By the early 1970s, 3,000-horsepower locomotives were the norm.

Alternating current traction motors were the next step in the power race. Direct current traction motors were poor at low speeds—in fact, they would burn up at less than 4 miles per hour under a heavy load. AC motors, on the other hand, would not burn out if the train stalled or moved slowly under heavy load for an extended time. Coal and other heavy commodities could be moved with fewer locomotives because it was no longer necessary to get speed up quickly.

The horsepower war took off in the late 1980s and early 1990s. Both EMD and GE stopped producing four-axle locomotives. Horsepower topped 4,000 and as the builders raced for 6,000, something no one anticipated happened: the railroads seemed to agree that 4,400 horsepower was plenty. When both builders perfected their 6,000-horsepower locomotives, demand was low.

Today, improvements are still being made to diesel technology. New manufacturers are filling in the holes that EMD and GE no longer address, such as four-axle passenger locomotives. Other companies are manufacturing hybrids to reduce fuel consumption and pollution. And the locomotive rebuilding market is booming as smaller railroads look for alternatives to new power. The last chapter in the development of the diesel won't be written for decades to come.

*Previous pages:* Railroading went through numerous changes in the 1980s and 1990s as lines merged and manufacturers introduced the "third generation" of diesel power. Norfolk Southern GE Dash 9-40C No. 9322 passes Conrail EMD SD60I No. 6721 shortly after NS took over Conrail.

# EMD F UNITS: REVOLUTIONARY FREIGHT POWER

Southern Railroad of New Jersey No. 728 was built in 1953, one of over 2,300 F7As built between 1949 and 1953. The unit wears the paint scheme of the New York, Ontario & Western (which ceased business in 1957).

Introduced in 1939, the FT produced 1,350 horsepower and could be configured in four-unit sets for a total output of 5,400 horsepower. With multiple-unit capability, one crew could operate any number of diesels, unlike steam locomotives, which required a full crew in each cab.

*Left:* The Reading Company owned eight FP7s to power passenger trains in eastern Pennsylvania. No. 902 was transferred to the Southeastern Pennsylvania Transportation Authority (SEPTA) after Reading discontinued passenger trains in the late 1970s.

*Below:* No. 413 was *reclassified* as an F10 after it was rebuilt from a Gulf, Mobile & Ohio F3 in 1979. Metro-North Railroad used a pair of F10s to augment its dual-powered FL9s. No. 413 also worked in Boston commuter service before going to Metro-North.

No. 578 was built in 1949 for the Chicago & North Western. An F7A, it later wound up in commuter service in New Jersey and New York before being painted as a Lehigh Valley locomotive for a New Jersey museum project.

The F unit was available as a cabless "B" or booster unit. A single A unit could control any number of B units to create as powerful a locomotive consist as was necessary. Many railroads put A units on each end of one or more B units to create a bi-directional locomotive set.

*Above:* Jersey Central F3A No. 56 leads F3B "D" in an "A-B" configuration, producing 3,000 horsepower. CNJ semipermanently coupled F3s and displayed the entire number on the lead unit—thus "56D." There is room for another number in case of an "A-B-A" configuration.

*Left:* Wabash No. 1189 was built by GMD (EMD's Canadian counterpart) in 1953. The F7A eventually became Norfolk & Western No. 3725 when the N&W leased the Wabash in 1964.

*Right:* Canadian Pacific FP7A was built by GMD in 1953 as CPR's No. 4099. It became No. 1400 in 1954 and was sold to VIA Rail in 1978 and then to the Nebkota Railroad in the U.S. in 1981 to haul freight. CPR repatriated old No. 4099 in 1998 for luxury passenger and business trains.

*Below:* Erie Mining (later LTV) used a fleet of F9s to haul iron ore in Minnesota until the mine closed in 2001. A not untypical locomotive consist included three or four F9Bs bracketed by F9As. The company owned five of each.

Clinchfield No. 800 started life in 1943 as an F3A but was later mechanically upgraded to an F7A. When Clinchfield was merged into Family Lines in the late 1970s, No. 800 received the scheme of its new owner. It later worked for CSX, successor to Family Lines.

| F UNIT PRODUCTION YEARS | | | |
|---|---|---|---|
| FT | 1939–1945 | 1,350 hp | 555 A units/541 B units |
| F2 | 1946 | 1,350 hp | 74 A units/30 B units |
| F3 | 1945–1949 | 1,500 hp | 1,111 A units/696 B units |
| F7 | 1949–1953 | 1,500 hp | 2,366 A units/1,483 B units |
| F9 | 1954–1957 | 1,750 hp | 87 A units/154 B units |

When the second-hand diesel market heated up in the 1970s, EMD introduced the GP15-1 as a new low-cost locomotive to compete with secondhand power. The new locomotive didn't really catch on, however. Only 310 units were sold between 1976 and 1982.

**The GP (General Purpose, sometimes colloquially referred to as "Geeps") series provided better visibility in both directions than did EMD's F units. Also, the lack of a full-cowl body gave maintenance forces easier access to the prime mover through a set of doors along both sides.**

*Above:* The GP9, such as Sierra No. 46, and its predecessor GP7 were two of EMD's biggest success stories. Introduced in 1949, the 1,500-horsepower GP7 sold 2,724 units. The GP9, rolled out in 1954, offered 1,750-horsepower and sold over 4,000 units.

*Left:* Boston & Maine No. 1732 is a GP9 built in 1957. GP7s and GP9s shared the same carbody with only the louver placement distinguishing them externally. No. 1732 now works for the Naugatuck Railroad, a museum operation in Connecticut.

Western Pacific GP20 No. 2001 and Southern Pacific GP9 No. 5623 were built seven years apart (1962 and 1955 respectively). The GP20 was EMD's first venture into turbocharging, boosting horsepower to 2,000.

**EARLY GP MODEL PRODUCTION**

| | | | |
|---|---|---|---|
| GP7 | 1949–1954 | 1,500 hp | 2,729 units |
| GP9 | 1954–1963 | 1,750 hp | 4,257 units |
| GP18 | 1959–1963 | 1,800 hp | 390 units |
| GP20 | 1959–1962 | 2,000 hp | 260 units |
| GP28 | 1964–1965 | 1,800 hp | 26 units |
| GP30 | 1961–1963 | 2,250 hp | 948 units |
| GP35 | 1963–1966 | 2,500 hp | 1,333 units |
| GP38 | 1966–1971 | 2,000 hp | 493 units |
| GP39 | 1969–1970 | 2,300 hp | 21 units |
| GP40 | 1965–1971 | 3,000 hp | 1,243 units |

*Above:* The GP30 continued the evolution of the GP series, increasing horsepower to 2,250. Southern Railway's GP30s were unusual for their high, short noses; most GP30s were delivered with a "chop" nose, permitting a windshield across the entire front of the locomotive.

*Left:* Reading Company GP30 No. 5513 has the more conventional chop nose found on later GPs. It was built in 1962, one of 20 GP30s purchased by the railroad and the first of 946 built by EMD.

The Pennsylvania Railroad owned 46 E7As, 25 E7Bs, and 74 E8As. E units were the backbone of the PRR's nonelectric passenger power, and some remained in service into the 1980s.

In 1937 and 1938, EMD introduced the EA, E1, and E2 stand-alone locomotives, all rated at 1,800 horsepower and all available in A and B units. A total of 29 units were constructed.

*Left:* The Erie Railroad rostered 14 E8As purchased in 1951 and used on the Erie's Hoboken-to-Chicago passenger trains. The railroad's passenger units wore an attractive two-tone green paint scheme, while cab units used for freight were painted black.

*Below:* The Delaware, Lackawanna & Western Railroad purchased 11 E8A's in 1951. The DL&W's premier passenger train, the *Phoebe Snow*, was one of the frequent assignments for the E8s.

While only 18 E3s (A and B units combined), 19 E4s, and 16 E5s were built, the E6 was widely accepted and 118 units were built. The E7 was even more successful, with 510 units built between 1945 and 1949.

The Burlington Route's E9s were bumped to commuter trains after Amtrak took over its intercity operations in 1971. The E9s became the queens of the "raceway," the triple-track main line from Chicago to Aurora, Illinois, where they served into the 1990s.

*Left:* New York, Susquehanna & Western's business train was powered by a pair of former Burlington E9s acquired when they were retired from Chicago commuter service. NYS&W No. 2402 had spent almost 50 years in Chicago commuter service.

Below: Conrail used a trio of E8s to power its business trains. Other railroads, such as Union Pacific and Illinois Central, did the same, while others used F units. Conrail's E8s came from its predecessors Erie-Lackawanna and Pennsylvania.

The E unit line received two more horsepower upgrades, first to 2,250 horsepower with the E8 in 1949 and then to 2,400 horsepower with the E9 starting in 1954. Some 460 E8s were built, along with 144 E9s. E unit production ended in 1965.

Southern Railway opted to stay out of Amtrak in 1971 and continued to operate its flagship train, the *Southern Crescent*, between New York and New Orleans. The Southern maintained a small fleet of E8s to power the train south of Washington, D.C.

*Above:* While the majority of E units had "bulldog" noses, the early models (E6 and before) had slanted noses. Atlantic Coast Line No. 501, an E6A built in 1939, is a classic example. ACL purchased 15 E6A and five E6B units.

*Left:* Union Pacific's E9A Nos. 949 and 951 bracket E8B No. 963 on company specials. All three units were acquired in 1955 and extensively rebuilt in 1993.

The RS-3 was the most popular Alco light road switcher, with over 1,300 units sold in the U.S. and Canada. New Haven No. 529 was an RS-3 built in 1952.

| ALCO RS PRODUCTION | | | |
|---|---|---|---|
| RS-1 | 1941–1946 | 1,000 hp | 417 units |
| RS-2 | 1946–1950 | 1,600 hp | 383 units |
| RS-3 | 1950–1956 | 1,600 hp | 1,370 units |

Vermont's Rutland Railway dieselized between 1950 and 1952 with the purchase of six RS-1s, nine RS-3s, and a GE 70-Ton locomotive. In 1964, the Rutland was divided into the Vermont Railway and the Green Mountain Railroad; two of the Alcos went to the Green Mountain, including No. 405.

The Batten Kill Railroad in New York uses Greenwich & Johnsonville RS-3 No. 4116, built in 1952 for the Delaware & Hudson, in freight service. RS-3 production lasted until 1956; interestingly, the last RS models built were RS-1s for Mexico in 1960.

## U.S. ALCO S PRODUCTION

| | | | |
|---|---|---|---|
| S-1 | 1940–1950 | 660 hp | 540 units |
| S-2 | 1940–1950 | 1,000 hp | 1,502 units |
| S-3 | 1950–1953 | 660 hp | 292 units |
| S-4 | 1950–1961 | 1,000 hp | 797 units |
| S-5 | 1954 | 800 hp | 7 units |
| S-6 | 1955–1960 | 900 hp | 126 units |

Kentucky & Tennessee No. 102 emerged from Alco in 1944, one of approximately 1,500 S-2s built by Alco. In addition, about 120 S models of various types were built in Canada by Montreal Locomotive Works.

*Above:* Similar in design to the S models was the T-6 ("T" for "transfer"). Rated at 1,000 horsepower, 59 were built. Middletown & Hummelstown No. 1016 was built in 1969 and was one of the last two locomotives built by Alco at Schenectady, New York.

*Left:* The Western Pacific rostered 8 S1s, 14 S2s, and 2 S4s purchased from Alco between 1942 and 1950. Stockton Terminal & Eastern purchased 10 of WP's switchers, using several into the late 1990s.

The Western Maryland purchased four FA-2s in 1951, including No. 303. It later went to the Long Island Rail Road where it served as a cab car. The unit now resides on the West Virginia Central, which has restored its WM paint scheme.

The FA-1 and its FB-1 booster counterpart were introduced in 1946 and received a horsepower boost in 1950. The FA-2 and FB-2 appeared in 1950, as did passenger models FPA-2 and FPB-2. The FPA-4 and FPB-4 were purchased only in Canada.

*Above:* The Long Island Rail Road purchased several FAs for cab car service on push-pull commuter trains. When the train operates in "push" mode, the engineer controls the train from the cab car in front while a locomotive on the rear of the train provides the power.

*Left:* Canadian National was the only purchaser of FPA-4s, which it used on passenger trains. No. 6789 was one of 36 FPA-4s CN bought between 1955 and 1959; it also purchased 14 FPB-4 booster locomotives.

*Right:* Nickel Plate No. 190 started life as Santa Fe 62L, a PA-1 built in 1948. It was sold to the Delaware & Hudson in 1967 and later to Mexico's national railway. It was repatriated by Doyle McCormack in 2000, who gave it the NKP livery.

*Below:* The Napa Valley Wine Train is one of the finest luxury dinner trains in the United States. A small fleet of pristine FPA-4s power the train through California's vineyards. No. 72 was originally CN No. 6787, built in 1959.

The PA was Alco's premier passenger power. Production ran from 1946 to 1953 across PA-1 and PA-2 models (as well as booster units for both). PA-1s produced 2,000 horsepower, while PA-2s produced 2,250. There were 297 PA and PB units built.

FPA-4s were transferred from Canadian National to VIA Rail when the latter assumed intercity passenger operations. After serving VIA, many FPA-4s found their way to tourist railroads. Cuyahoga Valley Scenic No. 15 wears a paint scheme inspired by the Delaware & Hudson.

Middletown & New Jersey No. 2 is a 44-Ton GE built in 1946. While most 44-Ton locomotives were used in industrial settings, the M&NJ used a pair to power freight trains over its 14-mile line in southern New York. GE ultimately built 373 44-Tonners.

GE created the 44-Ton locomotive in response to the "90,000 (45-ton) Rule" of 1937 that required a fireman on locomotives exceeding that weight. The 70-Tonner was designed for branch line service, but instead they found favor on short lines and in industrial settings.

*Left:* Modesto & Empire Traction maintains a fleet of 10 GE 70-Ton locomotives and continues to pick up additional 70-Tonners on the used locomotive market. The M&ET operates in California's Central Valley.

*Below:* Arcade & Attica uses a GE 65-Ton to power freights on its 15-mile railroad in western New York. No. 112 was built in 1945. The 65-Ton model was basically a 44-Tonner with a heavier frame and larger power plant.

California's Sierra Railroad used three Baldwin S-12s to power freights on an undulating line through the foothills. The S-12 was one of Baldwin's bestsellers, used for switching and short line applications. Sierra 40 and 42 were both built in 1955.

Unlike GE and EMD, Baldwin's roots were firmly planted in steam power. While EMD was revolutionizing motive power with the FT, Baldwin was forced by wartime restrictions to continue producing steam locomotives. By 1945, EMD had a huge jump on diesel design.

*Left:* When the Sierra needed a locomotive for its dinner train, it turned to Baldwin No. 42, which had been retired in the mid-1990s after 40 year of service. Sierra gave the veteran locomotive an overhaul and a facelift and returned it to active duty.

*Below:* The Amador Foothills Railroad, like other short lines, was tied directly to one major shipper: in this case, the paper mill at Martel, California. Baldwin S-12 No. 10 left Baldwin's Eddystone plant in 1951. In 2003 the Amador Foothills shut down permanently—for the second time.

Lima Locomotive Works was purchased by Baldwin in 1950. In 1951, all Lima diesel production ended after a mere 174 units. Whitewater Valley No. 25, a 750-horsepower switcher, was built in 1951 and is the only Lima diesel to operate in the new millennium.

Though the last Baldwins were built in 1956, some of the locomotives were still in service into the twenty-first century. Tough or not, there was just no challenging EMD and GE. Baldwins eventually were relegated to switcher and transfer service, where toughness was an asset.

*Above:* When SMS Rail Services began a switching operation in New Jersey, it accumulated the largest fleet of operating Baldwins in the country. First on the scene were two DS-4-4-10s, a 1,000-horsepower model of which Baldwin built almost 500 between 1946 and 1951.

*Left:* SMS brought three six-axle Baldwins AS-616s from the California desert to New Jersey. No. 554 was the only one of the three restored to operation by SMS. Baldwin built more than 150 of the model from 1950 to 1954.

| FIRST-GENERATION SD PRODUCTION | | | |
|---|---|---|---|
| SD7 | 1952–1953 | 1,500 hp | 188 units |
| SD9 | 1954–1959 | 1,750 hp | 471 units |
| SD18 | 1960–1963 | 1,800 hp | 54 units |
| SD24 | 1958–1963 | 2,400 hp | 224 units |
| SD28 | 1965 | 1,800 hp | 6 units |
| SD35 | 1964–1966 | 2,500 hp | 360 units |
| SDP35 | 1964–1965 | 2,500 hp | 35 units |
| SD38 | 1967–1971 | 2,000 hp | 53 units |
| SD38AC | 1971 | 2,000 hp | 15 units |

The Port of Tillamook Bay Railroad in Oregon, which accesses some of the most remote and rugged terrain in the state, picked up ten secondhand SD9s from Burlington Northern for its operation.

*Above:* The Algers, Winslow & Western, located in southwest Indiana, uses four second-hand SD9s to pull long, heavy coal trains. All four were built in 1955 for the Central of Georgia Railroad and were purchased by the AW&W to replace four-axle Alcos.

*Left:* The Duluth, Missabe & Iron Range in northern Minnesota began using six-axle EMD power with SD9s in the 1950s and SD18s in 1960. In the late 1960s the railroad purchased SD38s and SD38ACs (the difference being in the electrical system). DM&IR No. 185 is an SD18.

### FIRST-GENERATION SD PRODUCTION, continued

| | | | |
|------|-----------|----------|--------------|
| SD39 | 1968–1970 | 2,300 hp | 54 units |
| SDL39 | 1969–1972 | 2,300 hp | 10 units |
| SD40 | 1966–1972 | 3,000 hp | 1,275 units |
| SD40A | 1969–1970 | 3,000 hp | 18 units |
| SD45 | 1965–1971 | 3,600 hp | 1,260 units |

Great Northern No. 400, dubbed "Hustle Muscle," was EMD's first production 3,600-horsepower locomotive, rolling out of the shop in 1966. After 20 years on the GN and its successor Burlington Northern, it was donated to the Great Northern Historical Society.

Guilford Transportation No. 623 is designated an SD26, which wasn't an official EMD model. Santa Fe embarked on a SD24 rebuilding program between 1973 and 1978, with the locomotives receiving new prime movers and electrical systems. Many were sold to Guilford in 1986.

McCloud Railway No. 38 is an SD38 built in 1969, one of three purchased by the railroad. Dependent on lumber products, the McCloud ceased most operations in 2005 when its primary customer closed.

Two Metro-North FL9s rest at Danbury, Connecticut, at the end of the nonelectrified Danbury Branch. The dual-mode FL9s cruised the branch on diesel power, and outside Grand Central Terminal switched to electric current from a third rail.

The FL9 allowed the New Haven to operate into New York City's Grand Central Terminal without a time-consuming switch to electric locomotives outside of the city. Between 1956 and 1960 New Haven purchased 60 FL9s, the last of which were retired in 2005.

*Above:* Long after the New Haven Railroad was absorbed by Penn Central, the Connecticut Department of Transportation chose to paint its recently acquired secondhand FL9s in the New Haven's famed McGinnis scheme.

*Left:* Amtrak inherited some New Haven FL9s when it was formed in 1971, and it put them to use on the New York Central where they operated as diesels between Albany and Croton on Hudson. The locomotives were switched to electric power before entering Grand Central.

By the 1990s the number of operating Fairbanks-Morse locomotives could be counted on one hand. LTS No. 1845 was an H12-44 built for the U.S. Army in 1953. It later worked U.S. Steel's Failress Works in Pennsylvania, with most of its windows blanked out because of the hot furnaces.

A late-comer to the diesel market, Fairbanks-Morse was hampered by headaches caused by its opposed-piston engines. F-M exited the U.S. locomotive market in 1958, and ceased all railroad production in 1963 after building 1,460 opposed-piston locomotives.

*Left:* F-M was still in the marine business when North Carolina Ports approached them in 1996 about parts for two secondhand H12-44s. Not only were parts available, F-M offered to rebuild the engines. The result was two practically new F-Ms.

*Below:* F-M C-Liner production stopped in 1955; Train Masters remained in production until 1957. All of the C-Liners were ultimately scrapped and only one Train Master—Canadian Pacific No. 8905, built in 1955—escaped the scrapper's torch.

*Above:* Alcos were well-known for their thick exhaust. Here, Reading C-630 No. 5308 puts on quite a show. Reading purchased 10 C-424s in 1962 and 2 C-430s and 7 C-630s (including No. 5308) in 1966. An additional 5 C-630s were added in 1967.

*Right:* The Apache Railway in Arizona went all-Alco in 1962 with the purchase of three RS-32s. When the locomotives starting wearing out, the Apache purchased four C-424s from Canadian Pacific in 1998, including No. 99 (CPR's No.4233). The Apache also has four secondhand C-420s.

Alco introduced its Century line in 1963 with the 2,000-horsepower C-420 (the "420" referred to the number of axles [four] and hundreds of horsepower [20]). Other models included the C-424 (1963), C-425 (1964), C-430 (1966), C-628 (1963), C-630 (1965), and C-636 (1967).

Morristown & Erie's Alco roster lined up for a portrait on New Year's Eve 1995. Nos. 16 and 17 are C-430s built in 1967 for New York Central, while Nos. 18 and 19 are C-424s from 1964, built for the Toledo, Peoria & Western.

Chessie System U30B 8229 and two sisters head back toward the mines from Hinton, West Virginia. Chessie System consisted of three semi-independent roads: Chesapeake & Ohio, Baltimore & Ohio, and Western Maryland. No. 8229 was a C&O locomotive.

In 1959, the Universal Series propelled GE to within spitting distance of EMD. The U25B ("B" for four axles and "25" for 2,500 horsepower) was followed by the six-axle U25C in 1963. Horsepower increases resulted in the U28B and U28C in late 1965.

*Left:* GE U25B No. 2525 was the last locomotive purchased by the New Haven before it became a part of Penn Central in 1968. U25B production ran from 1955 to 1966; New Haven purchased 26 in 1964 and 1965.

*Below:* GE cranked out 465 U23Bs between 1968 and 1977, and 53 six-axle U23Cs between 1968 and 1970. The U23B was a response to demands for an intermediate-horsepower locomotive. Louisville & Nashville purchased 96 U23Bs between 1970 and 1975.

A pair of Family Lines U25Bs works DeCoursey Yard south of Covington, Kentucky. Family Lines was a short-lived amalgamation of several rail-roads. The railroads officially merged into the Seaboard System in 1982, which became a part of CSX in 1986.

New Jersey Department of Transportation purchased the only U-boats designed for passenger service. Its 32 U34CHs were based on the U36C freight locomotive, with 2,000 horsepower diverted for head-end power to supply electricity to passenger coaches.

Universal Series development continued with the introduction of the 3,000-horsepower U30B and U30C, as well as the U33B, in late 1966; the U33C in 1968; and the U36B and U36C in 1971. U-boat production ended in 1977.

The Southern Railway (and the Norfolk & Western) continued ordering locomotives with high short hoods long after most others had converted to the chopped hood for better visibility. Southern Railway No. 3961 is one of 70 U23Bs the railroad purchased.

The view from the roundhouse roof in Cranbrook, British Columbia, epitomizes the Canadian Pacific in the mid-1980s: SD40-2s as far as you could see. CPR was the third-largest purchaser of the model with 484 units.

The first of the EMD "Dash 2" models, the SD40-2 became nearly the universal six-axle freight locomotive of the late 1970s and early 1980s. By the time production ended in 1986, almost 4,000 had been built, along with over 300 "Tunnel Motor" SD40-2Ts.

*Above:* Union Pacific boasted the second-largest SD40-2 fleet, with 686 units purchased. SD40-2 production lasted from 1972 to 1986, with 21 U.S., 5 Canadian, and 2 Mexican railroads making purchases.

*Left:* Burlington Northern was the king of SD40-2 purchasers, picking up 779 copies. SD40-2s were well-suited for BN terrain, which ranged from the Columbia River in Washington State, to the Rockies in Montana, to the prairies in the upper Midwest.

# SD40-2: THE SECOND GENERATION BEGINS

Horseshoe Curve is the landmark location for the former Pennsylvania Railroad's climb through the Allegheny Mountains in its namesake state. Pennsy successor Conrail purchased 167 SD40-2s, many of which were used in helper service pushing trains over the mountains.

Externally, the Dash 2 series looks like typical EMD power produced up to the time of its introduction. Internally, however, transistors and circuit boards replaced hard-wired circuitry, making the Dash 2s extremely rugged and dependable.

*Left:* The "safety cab" locomotive, distinguished by its wide nose, was popular on the Canadian National long before it became almost universal on North American railroads. CN ordered 123 units, which became known as SD40-2Ws.

*Below:* Canadian Pacific's passage through the Selkirk Mountains in British Columbia features a climb over Rogers Pass. Mount MacDonald Tunnel, opened in 1988, eased the grades and eliminated the need for westbound trains to have six SD40-2 helpers added to the middle of the consist.

Burlington Northern's C30-7s were handsome machines in their Cascade-green paint. BN purchased over 200 of the six-axle 3,000-horsepower machines, and GE eventually built over 1,000, with BN's fleet being the largest in the U.S.

The Dash 7 series provided better tractive effort and fuel efficiency than U-boats. C30-7 production began in 1976; the first four-axle model, the B23-7, followed in 1977. Over 500 B23-7s were built, making it the most successful four-axle model of the series.

*Above:* The four-axle B30-7 and the six-axle C30-7 ushered in the Dash 7 series, keeping the classic external lines of the U-boats. Internal improvements, however, made the B30-7 GE's first second-generation diesel, while the externally similar U30C was the last of the first-generation.

*Left:* Conrail No. 1967 is an example of the most successful Dash 7 model, the B23-7. Conrail was the largest purchaser, buying 141 of the more than 500 units produced. No other U.S. railroad bought over 100 units, but Mexico's national railway picked up 114.

Grand Trunk Railway, a U.S. subsidiary of Canadian National, owned 86 GP38-2s, such as No. 5851, as well as 20 GP40-2s. While GP38-2s had 40 improvements over GP38s, the differences were largely internal.

The first production Dash 2 models were the four-axle GP38-2 and the six-axle SD40-2. More than 2,222 GP38-2s were built, along with over 1,000 GP40-2s. Dependability problems with the GP50 kept sales low, and the railroads kept buying the old reliable Dash 2s until 1984.

*Left:* The Richmond, Fredericksburg & Potomac used seven GP40-2s for its trains between Alexandria and Richmond, Virginia. Absorbed by CSX in 1991, RF&P had a unique signal system that required its locomotives to always lead trains.

*Below:* When Southern Pacific requested a better cooling system for its Dash 2 locomotives, EMD installed larger radiators, permitting locomotives to cool quicker before entering SP's short but numerous tunnels. There were 312 SD40T-2 and 249 SD45T-2 "Tunnel Motors" built.

*Right:* Amtrak purchased 210 F40PHs beginning in 1976. Covering virtually every intercity passenger assignment from the mid-1980s until the mid-1990s, as well as powering many commuter operations, the F40PH was truly North America's passenger locomotive.

*Below:* Caltrain, the commuter operator in the Bay Area, purchased 23 F40PH-2s for service between San Francisco and San Jose. The F40PH was originally designed as a short-haul locomotive, and commuter agencies in New Jersey, Illinois, and Ontario also bought them.

When created in 1971, Amtrak inherited a fleet of ragtag locomotives. Amtrak went shopping and settled on four-axle F40PHs for short-haul trains and six-axle SDP40Fs for long-haul trains. When the latter proved unsuccessful, the F40PH was pressed into long-distance service.

VIA Rail purchased 59 F40PH-2s, delivered between 1986 and 1989, to serve as their primary passenger locomotives. Although designated as F40PH-2s, the units are virtually identical to Amtrak's F40PHs.

In 1974 Metra, the commuter agency in the Chicago area, purchased 15 six-axle F40C commuter locomotives, basically passenger versions of the SD40-2.

The F40PH's only drawback seemed to be its head-end power generator that supplied electricity to the entire train. Because a passenger train always needs power, the locomotive's prime mover has to run full-throttle all the time. This resulted in heavy fuel consumption and a lot of noise.

*Left:* CSX Nos. 9992 and 9993 were originally built for Amtrak as the passenger carrier's Nos. 390 and 395. Other former Amtrak F40PHs eventually found their way to the Grand Canyon Railway and even the Panama Railroad.

*Below:* The final units in the F40 family were 30 F40PHM-2s built for Metra in 1991 and 1992. While the locomotives' guts were identical to the F40PH-2, the streamlined front end was dramatically different.

Chicago & North Western No. 8669 was purchased in 1994, one of an order of 127 Dash 9-44CWs. Bought to haul coal from the Powder River Basin, the C&NW's merger with Union Pacific found the prairie wanderers in exotic locations like Utah's Weber Canyon.

**When GE boosted horsepower from 3,900 on the C39-8 to 4,000, it renamed its locomotive line by leading with the word "Dash." The Dash 8-40C went into production in 1987 as GE's first 4,000-horsepower unit.**

*Above:* Norfolk Southern wasn't overly impressed with GE's upgrading of the Dash 9 series to 4,400 horsepower, instead ordering 856 safety cab–equipped units rated at 4,000 horsepower, the only Dash 9-40CWs built.

*Left:* Southern Pacific ordered 101 Dash 9-44CWs in 1994, and many found work on former Denver & Rio Grande lines acquired by the SP in 1984. Four SP units lead a freight down the Front Range of the Rockies outside Denver.

Once EMD proved AC technology was viable, GE wasted no time in developing its own AC locomotive. The result is the AC4400CW, basically an AC version of the Dash 9-44CW. GE's AC locomotives have gone on to outsell EMD's by a wide margin.

Distributed Power Units (DPUs) can be inserted either in the middle of a train or at the rear; in both cases, all the locomotives are controlled by the engineer in the lead locomotive. Canadian Pacific AC4400CW No. 9612 is a DPU. Here, it is running backwards in the middle of a heavy grain train headed for the Rockies.

*Left:* The Magnolia Cut-Off is one of the most spectacular rail lines in the East, cutting through mountains and across the Potomac River numerous times between Hancock and Paw Paw, West Virginia. CSX purchased No. 345 in 1998, one of 89 AC4400CWs the railroad bought that year.

*Below:* CSX has embraced GE's AC traction locomotives, purchasing almost 600 AC4400CWs and an additional 99 AC6000CWs. No. 11 is an AC4400CW purchased in 1994 as part of CSX's first order of the model.

Quebec Cartier Mining owns a remote railroad in eastern Quebec, hauling iron ore to the town of Port Cartier. The railroad purchased 12 AC4400CWs in 2002 to replace its aging fleet of Alco Centuries.

Union Pacific, so enthralled with the thought of a 6000-horsepower unit, placed a major order for GE's AC6000CW long before the model was ready. Since then, railroads have decided that 6,000-horsepower might not be the best idea due to maintenance issues.

*Left:* Canadian Pacific AC-4400CW No. 9130 emerges from Mount MacDonald Tunnel in British Columbia, the longest in North America. Where multiple SD40-2s once struggled to get a train over the hill, a single AC4400CW can power some intermodal trains over the Selkirks with ease.

*Below:* Canadian Pacific AC4400CW No. 9773 is decked out for the season as it powers the railroad's annual *Holiday Train*. The train began operations in 2002 to promote collecting food for the less fortunate, spreading cheer all along the CPR system.

While the locomotive is Conrail blue, the black patch under the cab indicates that this SD60M is part of Norfolk Southern's roster. The "M" signifies a wide-nose and "comfort" cab. Scioto Tower stood guard over this busy rail intersection in Columbus, Ohio, until 2005.

EMD introduced the 3,800-horsepower SD60 in 1984. Besides the new "710" series prime mover, SD60s were microprocessor-controlled, ushering in the unofficial third generation of diesel locomotives. SD60 sales were 1,138.

*Above:* Norfolk Southern SD60 No. 6638 has just descended Saluda Grade in North Carolina, the steepest main line grade in the United States. NS purchased over 160 SD60s between 1984 and 1991. Saluda Grade, always an operational headache, is now closed.

*Left:* Burlington Northern and successor BNSF Railway purchased over 800 SD70MACs, mostly to haul coal from Wyoming's Powder River Basin. The early BN SD70MACs received a unique dark-green and cream scheme that only they wore.

*Right:* EMD promoted its new SD90MAC by sending demonstration models around the country for railroads to test. SD90MAC No. 139 (actually equipped with a 4,300-horsepower prime mover, making it an SD9043AC) tested on the Vermont Rail System in 2000.

*Below:* Norfolk Southern purchased 56 SD70s with conventional cabs in 1993 and 1994, then went back and purchased 68 wide-nosed SD70Ms between 2000 and 2004. No. 2605, packing 4,000 horses, came to NS in 2003.

As GE and EMD raced to develop a 6,000-horsepower locomotive, EMD introduced the 5,000-horsepower SD80MAC in 1995 as an intermediate step. Alas, only 30 were purchased. The SD90MAC finally put 6,000-horsepower into an EMD locomotive.

Conrail was the only purchaser of the SD80MAC, EMD's 5,000-horsepower "interim" locomotive. Only 30 were built; more were on order for the Chicago & North Western, but Union Pacific's purchase of the C&NW canceled the order.

Amtrak No. 709 leads a train through Hudson, New York. The P32AC-DM is a 3,200-horsepower dual-mode unit capable of converting to electric power for its run through tunnels to Penn Station. Amtrak purchased 18 dual-mode locomotives from GE.

In the mid-1990s, Amtrak turned to GE for a locomotive that weighed less than the F40PH while delivering 1,000 more horse-power and fitting into the tunnels leading to New York City. GE responded with the Genesis series Dash 8-40BP, of which 46 were built.

*Left:* Amtrak P42DC No. 113 leads the *Coast Starlight* southbound between Seattle and Los Angeles. Much of the run south of San Francisco is within view of the Pacific Ocean, while the northern portion of the trip includes a spectacular crossing of Oregon's Cascade Mountains.

*Below:* Wearing the newest Amtrak paint scheme, blue-hooded P42DC No. 104 heads into Meriden, Connecticut, on Amtrak's Inland Route between New York and Boston. Amtrak purchased 208 P42DCs to replace F40PHs in most intercity service.

Metro-North purchased 31 P32AC-DMs for its service along the Hudson River, needing electric power for the trip through the Park Avenue Tunnel into New York's Grand Central Terminal. No. 201 glides through the Hudson mist near Peekskill, New York.

The Connecticut Department of Transportation purchased 10 P32AC-DMs as its contribution to Metro-North's service into Connecticut. CDOT decided to use the classic McGinnis scheme of the New Haven, a railroad that vanished in 1968.

Since GE upgraded the Dash 8-40BP to create the 4,200-horsepower P42DC, Amtrak has purchased over 200 of the new locomotives. VIA Rail, also faced with an aging locomotive fleet, has been a customer as well.

VIA Rail followed Amtrak into the new locomotive market, ordering 21 P42DCs. Unlike Amtrak, however, VIA has not used its new locomotives from coast to coast, but has confined them to the busy Toronto–Montreal corridor.

GO Transit (Government of Ontario) was the first buyer of the F59PH, working closely with EMD to design a more powerful replacement for the agency's F40PH fleet. No. 524 was among the first batch of 16 F59PHs delivered in 1998 and 1999.

When GO Transit convinced EMD to build a 3,000-horsepower passenger locomotive, EMD delivered the F59 and GO purchased 49 units. EMD found other buyers, including MetroLink for its Los Angeles–area commuter trains. In all, 79 F59PHs were built between 1988 and 1994.

*Left:* F59PHI No. 2004, arriving in Martinez, wears the unique "Amtrak California" paint scheme found on state-subsidized trains. Two decades earlier, Martinez had no passenger service. Over 30 trains now call at the town's station daily.

*Below:* MetroLink, the Los Angeles commuter train operator, purchased 23 F59PHs with conventional cabs, such as No. 852, in 1992 and 1993. An additional 14 F59PHIs ("I" for "isolated" cab) featuring a streamlined nose were added between 1995 and 2001.

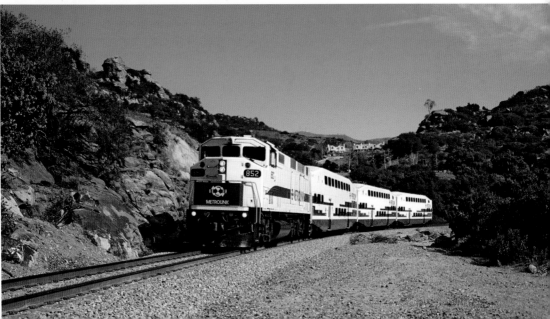

Amtrak purchased 21 F59PHIs for service in California in 1998. In cooperation with the state, Amtrak operates trains between Sacramento, San Jose, and Bakersfield. California also purchased 15 F59PHIs to augment Amtrak's units.

When Amtrak requested a F59PH with a rounded, streamlined front end, EMD answered with the F59PHI. MetroLink also ordered F59PHIs, as did commuter agencies in Seattle, Vancouver, Montreal, and North Carolina. In all, 74 F59PHI's have been built.

*Above:* The state of North Carolina financially supports two Amtrak trains operating between Raleigh and Charlotte and purchased two locomotives from EMD in 1998. *The City of Raleigh* and *The City of Charlotte* are Nos. 1755 and 1797, the respective years of the cities' founding.

*Left:* North Carolina maintains a small shop in Raleigh to service its two F59PHIs and a single GP40H-2. The F59PHI's round fiberglass nose has weathered a half-dozen grade-crossing collisions. Tragically, the same can't be said for the motorists who ignored the flashing lights.

With the Del Mar Race Track as a background, a Coaster commuter train races north from San Diego behind F40PH-2C No. 2102. North County Transit, operator of the Coaster, purchased five units in 1994.

**Locomotive rebuilder Morrison-Knudsen found itself in the new locomotive business in 1991 when the MBTA (Boston's commuter agency) purchased 9 copies of EMD's F40PH-2C. M-K has built 23 units in all.**

*Left:* Altamont Commuter Express purchased three F40PH-3Cs from Morrison-Knudsen when service between San Jose and Stockton, California, began in 1997. The service has proven so popular that two more locomotives were purchased in 2000 and another in 2005.

*Below:* At Del Mar, F40PH-2C No. 2101 takes commuters home high above the Pacific Ocean. Coaster trains terminate at Oceanside, which is also (not coincidentally) the southern terminus of Metro-Link commuter service out of Los Angeles.

Amtrak's last turbo train set rolls along the Hudson River on its way to New York City. Amtrak purchased seven turbo sets from Rohr Industries in 1976 and 1977. One survivor, rebuilt by Morrison-Knudsen, operated into the new millennium before being retired.

While turbo power had been experimented with off and on since the 1950s, the United States and Canada gave the technology another chance in the 1970s in an effort to compete with airlines on short-distance routes.

*Left:* United Aircraft sold eight TurboTrains to Penn Central and Canadian National in 1967. They were passed on to successors Amtrak and VIA Rail. The Canadian turbos never worked well and lasted until 1983. Amtrak had similar problems, and pulled the plugs in 1975.

*Below:* French manufacturer ANF sold Amtrak six turbo sets to be used in Chicago-area service. All were withdrawn from service by 1981. This one survives, albeit barely, in an Indiana junkyard more than 20 years after its last run.

Chicago's Metra purchased 23 MP36PH-3Cs in 2003 and another 4 in 2004. Tower A-2 controls Metra's busy intersection between its ex–Milwaukee Road line to Kenosha, Wisconsin, and its ex–Chicago & North Western line to Geneva, Illinois.

Metra, Caltrain, and the state of New Mexico turned to Morrison-Knudsen (now known as Motive Power Industries) for 3,600-horsepower streamlined locomotives. The first production units appeared in 2003.

*Left:* Caltrain MP36PH-3C No. 926 pushes a train into one of three tunnels the railroad uses out of San Francisco. All Caltrain trains operate with the locomotives on the south end—trains are pulled to San Jose and pushed to San Francisco.

*Below:* In conjunction with a major upgrading of its line between San Francisco and San Jose, Caltrain purchased six MP36PH-3Cs in 2003 for *Bullet Train* express service. Caltrain also purchased new coaches, added express tracks, and built new stations to cut travel times.

# INDEX